W9-BNL-072

MARGARET K. McELDERRY BOOKS • An imprint of Simon & Schuster Children's Publishing Division • 1230 Avenue of the Americas, New York, New York 10020 • Text copyright © 2018 by Maddie Johnson • Interior photographs copyright © 2018 by Maddie Johnson and Sonia Gates • Photos on pages 7,8,14,15 and 16 used with permission. • Jacket photographs copyright © 2018 by Sonia Gates • All rights reserved, including the right of reproduction in whole or in part in any form. • MARGARET K. McELDERRY BOOKS is a trademark of Simon & Schuster, Inc. • For information about special discounts for bulk purchases, please contact Simon & Schuster Special Sales at 1-866-506-1949 or business@simonandschuster.com. • The Simon & Schuster Speakers Bureau can bring authors to your live event. For more information or to book an event, contact the Simon & Schuster Speakers Bureau at 1-866-248-3049 or visit our website at www.simonspeakers.com. • Book design by Lauren Rille • The text for this book was set in Ariel Rounded. • Manufactured in China • 0718 SCP • First Edition • 10 9 8 7 6 5 4 3 2 1 • CIP data for this book is available from the Library of Congress. • ISBN 978-1-5344-3662-6 • ISBN 978-1-5344-3663-3 (eBook)

how TICKLES saved PICKLES

A TRUE STORY

by Maddie Johnson

Margaret K. McElderry Books • New York London Toronto Sydney New Delhi

My name is Pickles.
My parents say I'm
something special.

Maybe it's
because
I can
SURF.

Maybe it's
because
I can
PAINT.

Before I had a home of my own, I lived in a cold, flooded barn. All my brothers and sisters had been adopted.

ADOPT ME

I was the
last piglet left!

Until one day, my new parents arrived! They fell in love with my porky smile and my swirly snout, one half **PINK** and the other half **BLACK.**

They decided to rescue me.

They named me Pickles. I loved my new name,
just as much as I loved my new home.

I made so many
dog friends.
I could do
everything they
could do.

They said I am
something special.

One day I ate something I shouldn't have eaten.
I had to be rushed to the hospital!
"Pickles is very sick," the veterinarian said.
"He needs healthy blood."
But where would we find that?

Think! **Think!** Think!

Maybe another hog could help!
My parents searched high and low,
near and far for a pig with healthy
blood. They called friends and family.

FINALLY!

They found a pig for sale on a
faraway farm and rushed her to
the hospital.

When she arrived, what a
SURPRISE!
She was a massive 650-pound pig!
Now even for a pig, that's pretty
darn big.

My parents named her Tickles.
Tickles was here to share her blood
with me and save the day!

Thanks to my new blood, and a lot of bravery, I got better . . .

and better . . .

and better!

The vet said I was something special.

Sooeeeeeeey!

But what would
happen to Tickles?

She needed a safe forever home.
I remembered the flooded farm
and my own dreams of finding a
home. Tickles had saved me, so
I wanted to rescue her. But my
house was too small for Tickles to
stay there.

She wouldn't fit in my bathtub.

She wouldn't fit at our table.

And she **definitely** wouldn't fit in my bed.

My parents and I asked friends and family, neighbors and strangers, "Can anyone help find a home for Tickles?" We finally found a farm where Tickles could live freely and peacefully for the rest of her life.

The farmer promised to take good care of her, and I promised to come back for playdates.

Tickles was **HOME.**

I was happy for Tickles, but I knew I was going to miss her. I started to feel a little lonely. . . .

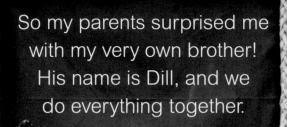

So my parents surprised me with my very own brother! His name is Dill, and we do everything together.

But our favorite thing to do is visit our best friend, Tickles.

People say I'm
something special,

but if you ask me . . .

Tickles is the most **special** pig of all.

When Pickles was five months old, he was taken to UC Davis Veterinary Hospital after becoming extremely ill. Unbeknownst to his parents, Pickles had found and eaten rat poison while they were travelling with him. Pickles was suffering from severe internal bleeding and desperately needed blood. The UC Davis Veterinary Hospital has one of the largest blood banks in the western United States (storing blood from dogs, cats, horses, goats, cows, llamas, sheep, and donkeys), but it does not store blood from pigs due to the difficulty of obtaining donations from them.

Pickles needed a blood transfusion within hours if he was to survive. The frantic search was on. Pickles's parents quickly found a 650-pound commercial pig for sale on Craigslist. After arranging for her transportation (which they also found on the site), they rushed the gigantic sow over to UC Davis. Pickles responded well to the multiple transfusions he received from the 650-pound hog-turned-hero, whom they eventually named Tickles.

Tickles's owner was selling her as a commercial butcher pig, but Pickles's owners grew incredibly attached to her and decided to purchase her the day she arrived. After calling many farms and sanctuaries, they finally found Tickles her forever home. She now lives happily at Veteran's Rescue Ranch in Hayward, California, where she greets visitors who come to the ranch and helps bring joy to the participants of their animal-assisted therapy program.

Pickles loves to visit Tickles on the weekends. He also loves volunteering as a therapy pig (or theraPIG as they call him); getting into mischief with his Frenchie brother, Dill; and hamming it up for the camera on social media. You can follow Pickles and his many adventures on Instagram and Facebook @livingwithpickles.

@livingwithpickles

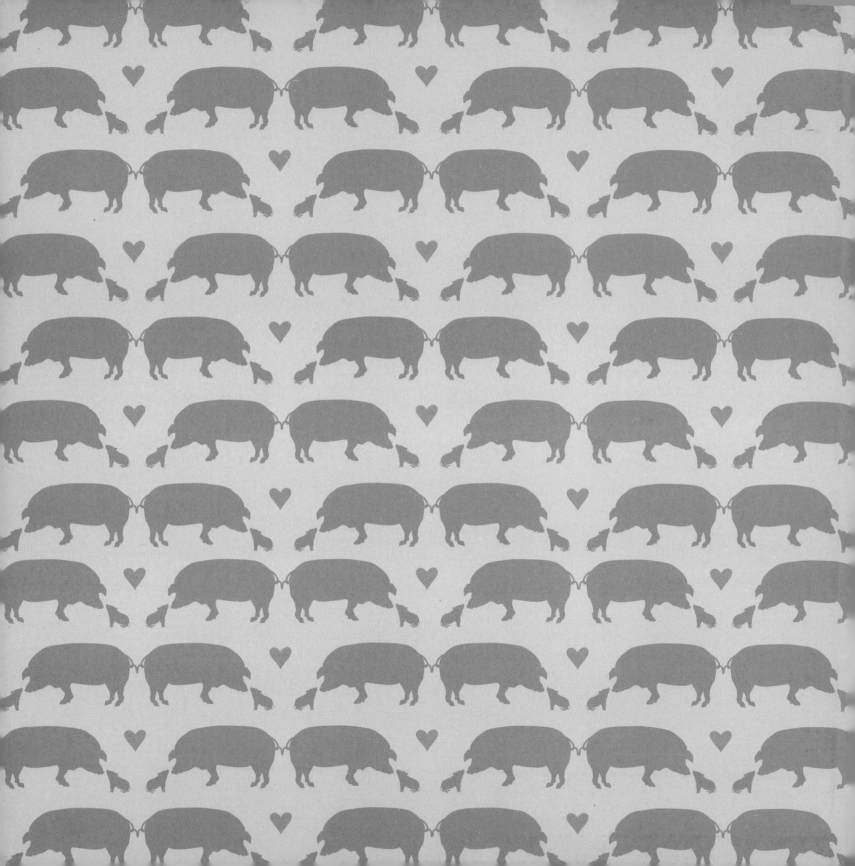